Lars

Cant .... you...

BLOOM!!!

THE STORY OF
THE WORLD'S
FIRST FLOWER

BLOOM

THE STORY OF THE WORLD'S FIRST FLOWER

ALEXANDER BRIAN MCCONDUIT

ILLUSTRATED BY CASSIA FRIELLO

BOOK DESIGN BY CASSIA FRIELLO

WWW.BIGBOOTBOOKS.COM
ISBN: 978-0-9851998-4-5

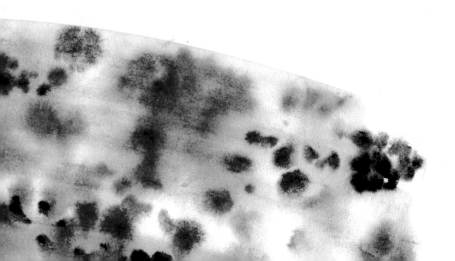

ACKNOWLEDGMENTS

THIS BOOK IS DEDICATED TO MY
GRANDMOTHER KATE MOLLAH, AND
TO THE WORLD'S FIRST FLOWER...
FOR IF YOU TWO NEVER EXISTED,
NEITHER WOULD I.

IN A TIME LONG BEFORE...

WHEN NOTHING ROAMED THE EARTH AND THE LAND WAS ROCKY AND BARE. ALL LIFE THAT EXISTED LIVED BENEATH THE SEA.

ALTHOUGH THE OCEANS
WERE FILLED WITH LIFE,
ABOVE THE SURFACE THERE
WERE NO BIRDS IN THE SKY,
NO BEASTS ON THE GROUND
AND NO BUGS IN THE DIRT.

BUT ALL OF THAT WAS ABOUT TO CHANGE...

SOMEWHERE, WE AREN'T
SURE EXACTLY WHERE
BUT SOMEWHERE NEAR A LAKE OR
A POND OR ON THE SHORES OF THE
OCEAN, PLANTS BEGAN LEAVING
THE SEA TO LIVE ON LAND.

NOT VERY WELL AT FIRST,
NOR FOR VERY LONG
BUT OVER TIME THESE PLANTS GOT
BETTER AND BETTER AT LIVING
ABOVE THE SURFACE.

AT FIRST THEY CAME
IN THE FORM OF ALGAE,
OR WHAT LOOKED LIKE
GREEN SLIME OR GOO.

OVER MILLIONS OF YEARS THIS
"GOO" EVOLVED SOME VERY
SPECIAL SKILLS AND GREW
SOME VERY SPECIAL PARTS TO
HELP IT SURVIVE.

THEY GREW STEMS

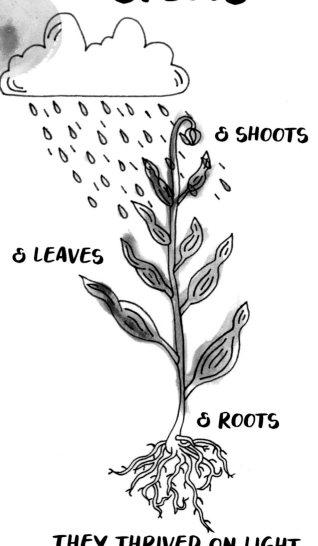

& SHOOTS

& LEAVES

& ROOTS

THEY THRIVED ON LIGHT
FROM THE SUN AND WATER
FROM THE RAIN

AND AS THE PLANTS LIVED, DIED AND DECAYED

MUCH OF THE LAND WAS CONVERTED INTO SOIL. THIS MADE THE WORLD AN EVEN BETTER PLACE FOR PLANTS TO BE!

AS TIME WENT ON THIS
LITTLE GREEN GOO, NOW
LOOKED A LOT MORE LIKE
THE PLANTS WE SEE TODAY.

WHAT'S EVEN MORE AMAZING IS
THAT THESE PLANTS EVENTUALLY
GREW EVERYWHERE!

AT ONE TIME, EARTH WAS COMPLETELY COVERED WITH BEAUTIFUL LUSH GREEN PLANTS.

SUNLIGHT

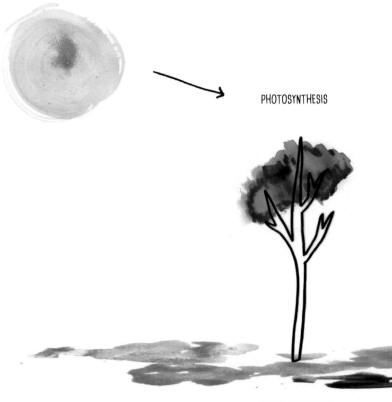

PHOTOSYNTHESIS

DECAY ORGANISMS

COOLING THE PLANET AS THEY TOOK IN CARBON DIOXIDE AND MAKING LIFE ON LAND POSSIBLE AS THEY RELEASED OXYGEN INTO THE ATMOSPHERE.

PLANTS BECAME ESSENTIAL TO LIFE ON LAND

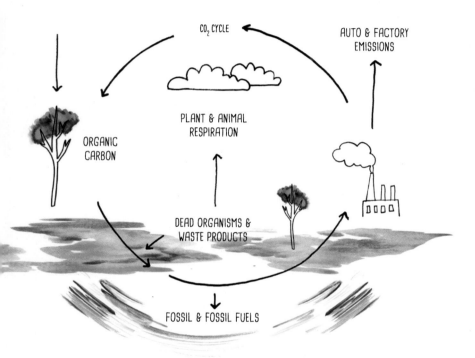

CO$_2$ CYCLE

AUTO & FACTORY EMISSIONS

PLANT & ANIMAL RESPIRATION

ORGANIC CARBON

DEAD ORGANISMS & WASTE PRODUCTS

FOSSIL & FOSSIL FUELS

PROVIDING FOOD, WATER AND SHELTER FOR MANY OF NATURE'S CREATURES. SOON, HOWEVER, PLANTS WERE ABOUT TO GIVE NATURE EVEN MORE.

ONE DAY, SOMETHING
NEW BEGAN TO GROW,
IT WASN'T A ROOT, OR A BRANCH,
OR A TRUNK, OR A LEAF. WELL
ACTUALLY, IT WAS A LEAF, BUT IT
WAS DIFFERENT FROM EVERY OTHER
LEAF BEFORE IT.

IT WAS THE WORLDS FIRST FLOWER!

IT WAS COLORFUL, SMELLED SWEET
AND HAD NEVER EXISTED BEFORE!

AS THE SUN ROSE,
THE PETALS OF THE FLOWER
BEGAN TO UNFOLD!

BUT THEN...
JUST LIKE THAT!
IT SHRIVELED UP, DIED
AND FELL TO THE FLOOR.

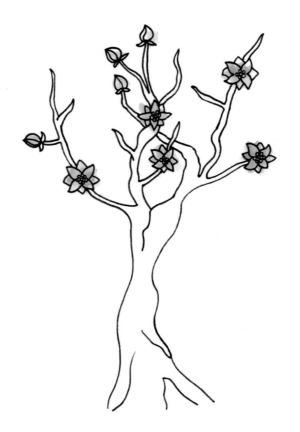

AFTER SOME TIME,
ANOTHER FLOWER
APPEARED.
IT WAS BIGGER AND SMELLED
SWEETER THAN THE FLOWER
BEFORE. IT WAS STRONGER AND
LIVED LONGER...

BUT THEN...
THE FLOWER SHRIVELED UP
AND FELL TO THE FLOOR.

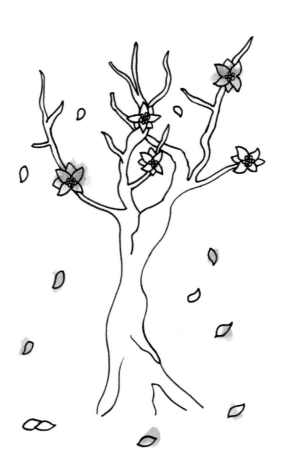

AND THEN THERE
WERE NO MORE
FLOWERS.

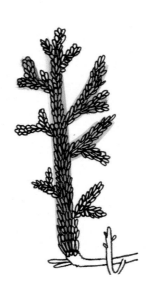

AROUND THE WORLD,
EVERY NOW AND
THEN, A FLOWER WOULD
APPEAR IN A BUSH, OR ON
A PLANT OR IN A TREE.
SOMETIMES HERE, OTHER
TIMES THERE.

SOMETIMES FOUR
AT A TIME, OTHER
TIMES JUST ONE.

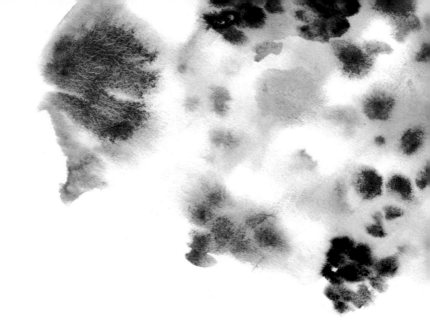

MOST TIMES
NONE
AT ALL.

BUT ONE DAY,

WHEN THE AIR WAS JUST
RIGHT AND THE SUN WAS
READY TO SHINE ON THEIR
PETALS AND THE PLANTS
WERE FULL FROM THE
RAINS AND THE WIND
COULD CARRY THEIR SCENT
AND NATURE COULD DRINK
THEIR NECTAR, ALL OF THE
WORLD'S FLOWERS OPENED
UP AT ONCE!!!!

EVER SINCE THAT DAY, PLANTS HAVE SHARED THEIR FLOWERS WITH THE WORLD.

GIVING ITS NECTAR TO THE HUMMING BIRDS AND ITS POLLEN TO THE BEES, DRASTICALLY TRANSFORMING LIFE ON OUR PLANET AS WE KNOW IT.

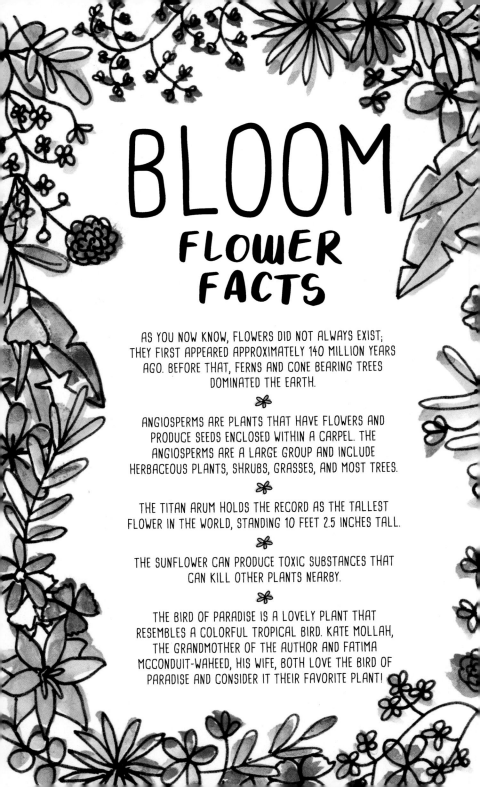

BLOOM
FLOWER FACTS

AS YOU NOW KNOW, FLOWERS DID NOT ALWAYS EXIST; THEY FIRST APPEARED APPROXIMATELY 140 MILLION YEARS AGO. BEFORE THAT, FERNS AND CONE BEARING TREES DOMINATED THE EARTH.

✿

ANGIOSPERMS ARE PLANTS THAT HAVE FLOWERS AND PRODUCE SEEDS ENCLOSED WITHIN A CARPEL. THE ANGIOSPERMS ARE A LARGE GROUP AND INCLUDE HERBACEOUS PLANTS, SHRUBS, GRASSES, AND MOST TREES.

✿

THE TITAN ARUM HOLDS THE RECORD AS THE TALLEST FLOWER IN THE WORLD, STANDING 10 FEET 2.5 INCHES TALL.

✿

THE SUNFLOWER CAN PRODUCE TOXIC SUBSTANCES THAT CAN KILL OTHER PLANTS NEARBY.

✿

THE BIRD OF PARADISE IS A LOVELY PLANT THAT RESEMBLES A COLORFUL TROPICAL BIRD. KATE MOLLAH, THE GRANDMOTHER OF THE AUTHOR AND FATIMA MCCONDUIT-WAHEED, HIS WIFE, BOTH LOVE THE BIRD OF PARADISE AND CONSIDER IT THEIR FAVORITE PLANT!

FLOWER PARTS

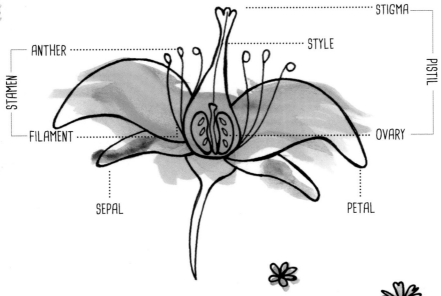

STIGMA

STYLE

ANTHER

STAMEN

PISTIL

FILAMENT

OVARY

SEPAL

PETAL

Made in the USA
Monee, IL
21 March 2024

55001817R00026